Crunchy Creations

The Ultimate Potato Chips Cookbook

While every precaution has been taken in the preparation of this book, the publisher assumes no responsibility for errors or omissions, or for damages resulting from the use of the information contained herein.

CRUNCHY CREATIONS

First edition. February 13, 2024.

ISBN: 979-8224185252

Written by Jose Maria.

Table of Contents

Jose Maria

❖ Introduction

A. Brief History of Potato Chips

Potato chips, a beloved snack enjoyed worldwide, have a fascinating origin dating back to the 19th century. Legend has it that the first potato chips were created in Saratoga Springs, New York, in 1853. A frustrated diner, complaining about thick and soggy fried potatoes, prompted chef George Crum to thinly slice potatoes, fry them to a crisp, and season them generously with salt. To the diner's surprise, these thin, crispy potatoes became an instant hit, eventually gaining popularity across the United States and beyond.

B. Importance of Homemade Potato Chips

While store-bought potato chips are convenient, homemade potato chips offer a level of freshness, flavor customization, and control over ingredients that cannot be matched. By making potato chips at home, you can experiment with various seasonings, ensure the use of quality ingredients, and tailor the chips to your taste preferences. Additionally, homemade potato chips can be a fun and rewarding culinary endeavor, allowing you to showcase your creativity in the kitchen while impressing friends and family with your crunchy creations.

C. Tips for Perfecting Homemade Potato Chips

1. Choose the Right Potatoes: Opt for high-starch potatoes like Russets or Yukon Golds, as they yield the crispiest results. Avoid waxy potatoes, as they tend to become soggy when fried.

2. Slice Uniformly: Consistent slicing ensures even cooking. Use a mandoline slicer or a sharp knife to cut the potatoes into thin, uniform slices, approximately 1/16 to 1/8 inch thick.

3. Soak in Cold Water: After slicing, soak the potato slices in cold water for at least 30 minutes to remove excess starch. This helps prevent the chips from sticking together during frying and promotes a crispier texture.

4. Dry Thoroughly: Before frying, pat the potato slices dry with paper towels to remove excess moisture. This step is crucial for achieving crispy chips.

5. Maintain Oil Temperature: Fry the potato chips in batches at the correct oil temperature, typically around 350°F (175°C). Avoid overcrowding the frying vessel, as this can lower the oil temperature and result in greasy chips.

6. Season Immediately: Season the freshly fried potato chips with your desired seasonings while they are still hot and oily. This allows the seasonings to adhere better to the chips, enhancing their flavor.

7. Cool and Drain: Transfer the seasoned potato chips to a wire rack set over a baking sheet to cool and drain excess oil. This helps preserve their crispiness and prevents them from becoming soggy.

With these tips in mind, you'll be well on your way to mastering the art of homemade potato chips and delighting your taste buds with irresistible crunchiness.

Chapter (1) Getting Started

A. Essential Equipment and Ingredients

Equipment:

1. Mandoline slicer or sharp knife
2. Large bowl
3. Colander
4. Paper towels
5. Deep-fry thermometer
6. Spider skimmer or slotted spoon
7. Wire rack set over a baking sheet

Ingredients:

1. Potatoes (Russet or Yukon Gold)
2. Vegetable oil or peanut oil for frying
3. Salt (for classic potato chips)
4. Additional seasonings and spices (for flavored potato chips)
5. Optional: Truffle oil, Parmesan cheese, rosemary, sea salt, barbecue seasoning, sour cream and onion seasoning, vinegar, garlic, herbs, lime, chili powder, masala spices, wasabi powder, soy sauce, sweet potatoes, assorted vegetables (for alternative chip varieties)

B. Selecting the Right Potatoes

Choosing the right type of potato is crucial for achieving crispy and flavorful homemade potato chips. Opt for high-starch potatoes, such as Russets or Yukon Golds, which have a low moisture content and are ideal for frying. These varieties produce chips with a light and crispy texture. Avoid waxy potatoes, as they tend to retain moisture and can result in soggy chips.

C. Preparing Potatoes for Slicing

1. Wash and Scrub: Thoroughly wash and scrub the potatoes under cold running water to remove any dirt or debris. Use a vegetable brush if necessary.

2. Peel (Optional): Depending on your preference, you can choose to peel the potatoes or leave the skins intact. Peeling the potatoes will result in a smoother texture, while leaving the skins on adds a rustic appearance and additional nutrients.

3. Slice Uniformly: Using a mandoline slicer or a sharp knife, slice the potatoes into thin, uniform rounds. Aim for slices that are approximately 1/16 to 1/8 inch thick. Consistent slicing ensures even cooking and crispy results.

4. Soak in Cold Water: Place the sliced potatoes in a large bowl filled with cold water. Soak them for at least 30 minutes to remove excess starch. This step helps prevent the chips from sticking together during frying and promotes crispiness.

5. Drain and Dry: After soaking, drain the potato slices in a colander and pat them dry thoroughly with paper towels. Removing excess moisture is essential for achieving crispy chips during frying.

With your potatoes prepared and ready for slicing, you're now equipped to embark on your homemade potato chip-making journey.

Chapter (2) Classic Potato Chip Recipes

A. Salted Potato Chips
Ingredients:

- 2 large Russet potatoes, thinly sliced
- Vegetable oil for frying
- Salt, to taste

Instructions:

1. Heat vegetable oil in a deep fryer or large pot to 350°F (175°C).
2. Carefully add a handful of potato slices to the hot oil, ensuring they are not overcrowded.
3. Fry the potato slices in batches for 3-4 minutes or until golden brown and crispy.
4. Using a spider skimmer or slotted spoon, transfer the fried chips to a wire rack set over a baking sheet to drain excess oil.
5. Immediately sprinkle the hot chips with salt to taste while they are still oily.
6. Repeat frying process with remaining potato slices.
7. Allow the salted potato chips to cool completely before serving. Enjoy the crispy goodness!

B. Barbecue Potato Chips
Ingredients:

- 2 large Russet potatoes, thinly sliced
- Vegetable oil for frying
- Barbecue seasoning or spice rub

Instructions:

1. Follow steps 1-4 from the Salted Potato Chips recipe to fry and

drain the potato slices.

2. While the chips are still hot and oily, sprinkle them generously with barbecue seasoning or spice rub, coating both sides evenly.

3. Gently toss the seasoned chips to ensure the seasoning is distributed evenly.

4. Allow the barbecue potato chips to cool before serving. Enjoy the smoky and savory flavor!

C. Sour Cream and Onion Potato Chips

Ingredients:

- 2 large Russet potatoes, thinly sliced
- Vegetable oil for frying
- Sour cream and onion seasoning mix

Instructions:

1. Follow steps 1-4 from the Salted Potato Chips recipe to fry and drain the potato slices.

2. While the chips are still hot and oily, sprinkle them generously with sour cream and onion seasoning mix, coating both sides evenly.

3. Gently toss the seasoned chips to ensure the seasoning is distributed evenly.

4. Allow the sour cream and onion potato chips to cool before serving. Enjoy the tangy and savory flavor!

D. Salt and Vinegar Potato Chips

Ingredients:

- 2 large Russet potatoes, thinly sliced
- Vegetable oil for frying
- White vinegar
- Salt

Instructions:

1. Follow steps 1-4 from the Salted Potato Chips recipe to fry and drain the potato slices.
2. In a small bowl, mix together equal parts white vinegar and water.
3. While the chips are still hot and oily, lightly sprinkle them with salt.
4. Using a spray bottle or pastry brush, lightly mist or brush the hot chips with the vinegar-water mixture.
5. Allow the salt and vinegar potato chips to cool before serving. Enjoy the tangy and salty flavor combination!

These classic potato chip recipes are sure to satisfy your crunchy cravings. Experiment with different seasonings and enjoy the delicious results!

Chapter (3) Gourmet Potato Chip Varieties

A. Truffle Oil and Parmesan Potato Chips
Ingredients:

- 2 large Russet potatoes, thinly sliced
- Vegetable oil for frying
- Truffle oil
- Grated Parmesan cheese
- Salt, to taste

Instructions:

1. Follow steps 1-4 from the Salted Potato Chips recipe to fry and drain the potato slices.
2. While the chips are still hot and oily, drizzle them lightly with truffle oil.
3. Sprinkle the chips generously with grated Parmesan cheese and salt to taste.
4. Gently toss the chips to ensure the truffle oil and Parmesan are evenly distributed.
5. Allow the truffle oil and Parmesan potato chips to cool before serving. Enjoy the luxurious flavor!

B. Rosemary and Sea Salt Potato Chips
Ingredients:

- 2 large Russet potatoes, thinly sliced
- Vegetable oil for frying
- Fresh rosemary, finely chopped
- Coarse sea salt

Instructions:

1. Follow steps 1-4 from the Salted Potato Chips recipe to fry and drain the potato slices.
2. While the chips are still hot and oily, sprinkle them generously with chopped fresh rosemary and coarse sea salt.
3. Gently toss the chips to ensure the rosemary and sea salt are evenly distributed.
4. Allow the rosemary and sea salt potato chips to cool before serving. Enjoy the fragrant and savory flavor!

C. Sriracha Lime Potato Chips
Ingredients:

- 2 large Russet potatoes, thinly sliced
- Vegetable oil for frying
- Sriracha sauce
- Fresh lime juice
- Salt, to taste

Instructions:

1. Follow steps 1-4 from the Salted Potato Chips recipe to fry and drain the potato slices.
2. While the chips are still hot and oily, drizzle them lightly with Sriracha sauce.
3. Squeeze fresh lime juice over the chips and sprinkle them with salt to taste.
4. Gently toss the chips to ensure the Sriracha and lime flavors are evenly distributed.
5. Allow the Sriracha lime potato chips to cool before serving. Enjoy the spicy and tangy kick!

D. Pesto and Sundried Tomato Potato Chips

Ingredients:

- 2 large Russet potatoes, thinly sliced
- Vegetable oil for frying
- Pesto sauce
- Chopped sundried tomatoes
- Salt, to taste

Instructions:

1. Follow steps 1-4 from the Salted Potato Chips recipe to fry and drain the potato slices.
2. While the chips are still hot and oily, drizzle them lightly with pesto sauce.
3. Sprinkle chopped sundried tomatoes over the chips and season with salt to taste.
4. Gently toss the chips to ensure the pesto and sundried tomato flavors are evenly distributed.
5. Allow the pesto and sundried tomato potato chips to cool before serving. Enjoy the vibrant and savory flavor combination!

These gourmet potato chip varieties are perfect for elevating snack time or impressing guests at your next gathering. Enjoy the delicious and unique flavors!

Chapter (4) Ethnic-Inspired Potato Chip Recipes

A. Spicy Masala Potato Chips (Indian)
Ingredients:

- 2 large Russet potatoes, thinly sliced
- Vegetable oil for frying
- 1 tablespoon garam masala
- 1 teaspoon chili powder
- 1/2 teaspoon turmeric powder
- Salt, to taste

Instructions:

1. Follow steps 1-4 from the Salted Potato Chips recipe to fry and drain the potato slices.
2. In a small bowl, combine garam masala, chili powder, turmeric powder, and salt.
3. While the chips are still hot and oily, sprinkle them generously with the masala spice mixture.
4. Gently toss the chips to ensure the spices are evenly distributed.
5. Allow the spicy masala potato chips to cool before serving. Enjoy the bold and flavorful taste of India!

B. Garlic and Herb Potato Chips (Mediterranean)
Ingredients:

- 2 large Russet potatoes, thinly sliced
- Vegetable oil for frying
- 2 cloves garlic, minced
- 2 tablespoons fresh herbs (such as rosemary, thyme, or oregano), finely chopped

- Salt, to taste

Instructions:

1. Follow steps 1-4 from the Salted Potato Chips recipe to fry and drain the potato slices.
2. In a small bowl, combine minced garlic, fresh herbs, and salt.
3. While the chips are still hot and oily, sprinkle them generously with the garlic and herb mixture.
4. Gently toss the chips to ensure the garlic and herbs are evenly distributed.
5. Allow the garlic and herb potato chips to cool before serving. Enjoy the aromatic flavors of the Mediterranean!

C. Wasabi and Soy Sauce Potato Chips (Japanese)
Ingredients:

- 2 large Russet potatoes, thinly sliced
- Vegetable oil for frying
- Wasabi paste
- Soy sauce
- Sesame seeds (optional)
- Salt, to taste

Instructions:

1. Follow steps 1-4 from the Salted Potato Chips recipe to fry and drain the potato slices.
2. While the chips are still hot and oily, drizzle them lightly with soy sauce.
3. Add small dollops of wasabi paste over the chips, distributing evenly.
4. Optional: Sprinkle sesame seeds over the chips for extra flavor and texture.

5. Allow the wasabi and soy sauce potato chips to cool before serving. Enjoy the bold and savory taste of Japan!

D. Chili Lime Potato Chips (Mexican)
Ingredients:

- 2 large Russet potatoes, thinly sliced
- Vegetable oil for frying
- Chili powder
- Lime zest
- Fresh lime juice
- Salt, to taste

Instructions:

1. Follow steps 1-4 from the Salted Potato Chips recipe to fry and drain the potato slices.
2. In a small bowl, combine chili powder and lime zest.
3. While the chips are still hot and oily, sprinkle them generously with the chili powder and lime zest mixture.
4. Drizzle fresh lime juice over the chips and sprinkle with salt to taste.
5. Gently toss the chips to ensure the flavors are evenly distributed.
6. Allow the chili lime potato chips to cool before serving. Enjoy the zesty and tangy taste of Mexico!

These ethnic-inspired potato chip recipes offer a delicious twist on traditional flavors from around the world. Enjoy exploring new taste sensations with these crunchy creations!

Chapter (5) Healthier Alternatives

A. Baked Potato Chips
Ingredients:

- 2 large Russet potatoes, thinly sliced
- Olive oil
- Salt, to taste
- Optional: herbs or spices of your choice

Instructions:

1. Preheat the oven to 400°F (200°C). Line a baking sheet with parchment paper.
2. Place the thinly sliced potatoes in a single layer on the prepared baking sheet.
3. Lightly brush both sides of the potato slices with olive oil.
4. Sprinkle salt and any desired herbs or spices over the potato slices.
5. Bake in the preheated oven for 15-20 minutes, flipping the slices halfway through, until the chips are golden brown and crispy.
6. Remove from the oven and allow the baked potato chips to cool slightly before serving. Enjoy the healthier alternative to traditional fried chips!

B. Sweet Potato Chips
Ingredients:

- 2 large sweet potatoes, thinly sliced
- Olive oil
- Salt, to taste
- Optional: cinnamon or other sweet spices

Instructions:

1. Preheat the oven to 375°F (190°C). Line a baking sheet with parchment paper.
2. Place the thinly sliced sweet potatoes in a single layer on the prepared baking sheet.
3. Lightly brush both sides of the sweet potato slices with olive oil.
4. Sprinkle salt and any desired sweet spices over the sweet potato slices.
5. Bake in the preheated oven for 20-25 minutes, flipping the slices halfway through, until the chips are crispy and lightly browned.
6. Remove from the oven and allow the sweet potato chips to cool slightly before serving. Enjoy the nutritious and flavorful snack!

C. Veggie Chips with a Potato Base
Ingredients:

- 2 large potatoes, thinly sliced
- Assorted vegetables (such as carrots, beets, zucchini), thinly sliced
- Olive oil
- Salt, to taste
- Optional: herbs or spices of your choice

Instructions:

1. Preheat the oven to 375°F (190°C). Line a baking sheet with parchment paper.
2. Place the thinly sliced potatoes and assorted vegetables in a single layer on the prepared baking sheet.
3. Lightly brush both sides of the vegetable slices with olive oil.
4. Sprinkle salt and any desired herbs or spices over the slices.
5. Bake in the preheated oven for 20-25 minutes, flipping the

slices halfway through, until the chips are crispy and lightly browned.

6. Remove from the oven and allow the veggie chips to cool slightly before serving. Enjoy the colorful and nutritious snack!

D. Air-fried Potato Chips
Ingredients:

- 2 large Russet potatoes, thinly sliced
- Olive oil spray
- Salt, to taste
- Optional: herbs or spices of your choice

Instructions:

1. Preheat the air fryer to 375°F (190°C) for 3-5 minutes.
2. Place the thinly sliced potatoes in a single layer in the air fryer basket.
3. Lightly spray the potato slices with olive oil spray.
4. Sprinkle salt and any desired herbs or spices over the potato slices.
5. Air fry the potato slices for 12-15 minutes, shaking the basket halfway through, until the chips are crispy and golden brown.
6. Remove from the air fryer and allow the potato chips to cool slightly before serving. Enjoy the crunchy and healthier alternative to traditional fried chips!

These healthier alternatives to traditional potato chips offer delicious options for satisfying your snack cravings while still being mindful of your health. Enjoy experimenting with different flavors and combinations!

Chapter (6) Creative Uses for Potato Chips

A. Crunchy Toppings for Salads
Ingredients:

- Fresh salad greens of your choice
- Assorted vegetables (tomatoes, cucumbers, bell peppers, etc.)
- Potato chips, crushed

Instructions:

1. Prepare your favorite salad with fresh greens and assorted vegetables.
2. Just before serving, sprinkle crushed potato chips over the top of the salad for added crunch and flavor.
3. Toss lightly to incorporate the chips into the salad.
4. Serve immediately and enjoy the crispy texture contrast in your salad!

B. Potato Chip Crusted Chicken Tenders
Ingredients:

- Chicken breast tenders or strips
- Flour
- Eggs, beaten
- Potato chips, crushed
- Salt and pepper, to taste
- Cooking oil for frying or baking

Instructions:

1. Preheat the oven to 400°F (200°C) if baking or heat oil in a

skillet for frying.

2. Season the chicken tenders with salt and pepper.
3. Dredge each chicken tender in flour, then dip into beaten eggs, and finally coat with crushed potato chips.
4. For baking: Place the coated chicken tenders on a baking sheet lined with parchment paper. Bake for 15-20 minutes or until golden brown and cooked through.
5. For frying: Fry the coated chicken tenders in hot oil until golden brown and cooked through, about 3-4 minutes per side.
6. Serve the potato chip crusted chicken tenders with your favorite dipping sauce and enjoy the crunchy exterior and tender chicken inside!

C. Potato Chip Trail Mix
Ingredients:

- Assorted nuts (almonds, cashews, peanuts)
- Dried fruits (raisins, cranberries, apricots)
- Chocolate chips or chunks
- Potato chips, crushed

Instructions:

1. In a large bowl, combine the assorted nuts, dried fruits, chocolate chips, and crushed potato chips.
2. Toss gently to mix all the ingredients evenly.
3. Portion the trail mix into individual servings or store in an airtight container for later snacking.
4. Enjoy the sweet, salty, and crunchy combination of flavors in this unique trail mix!

D. Chocolate Covered Potato Chips
Ingredients:

- Potato chips
- Chocolate chips or melting chocolate
- Optional: sprinkles, crushed nuts, sea salt

Instructions:

1. Melt the chocolate chips or melting chocolate according to package instructions.
2. Dip each potato chip halfway into the melted chocolate, allowing any excess chocolate to drip off.
3. Place the chocolate-covered potato chips on a parchment-lined baking sheet.
4. Optional: Sprinkle with toppings like sprinkles, crushed nuts, or a pinch of sea salt while the chocolate is still wet.
5. Allow the chocolate to set completely at room temperature or in the refrigerator.
6. Once set, store the chocolate-covered potato chips in an airtight container until ready to enjoy. Indulge in the irresistible combination of sweet chocolate and salty potato chips!

These creative uses for potato chips offer a fun and delicious way to enjoy this crunchy snack in unexpected ways. Experiment with different combinations and get creative in the kitchen!

Chapter (7) Serving Suggestions and Pairings

A. Dips and Sauces
Classic Potato Chips:

- Serve with traditional dips such as ranch, French onion, or sour cream and chive.
- Experiment with homemade dips like creamy garlic aioli, tangy barbecue sauce, or spicy salsa.

Flavored Potato Chips:

- Match Salt and Vinegar Potato Chips with a creamy dill dip.
- Pair Barbecue Potato Chips with a smoky chipotle mayonnaise.
- Accompany Sour Cream and Onion Potato Chips with a tangy Greek yogurt dip.

Gourmet Potato Chips:

- Complement Truffle Oil and Parmesan Potato Chips with a balsamic reduction dip.
- Serve Rosemary and Sea Salt Potato Chips with a roasted garlic hummus.
- Pair Sriracha Lime Potato Chips with a cool cucumber tzatziki sauce.
- Match Pesto and Sundried Tomato Potato Chips with a basil pesto mayo.

B. Beverages
Classic Potato Chips:

- Enjoy with a cold and refreshing soda, such as cola or lemon-lime.
- Pair with a light lager or pilsner beer for a classic combination.

Flavored Potato Chips:

- Pair Salt and Vinegar Potato Chips with a crisp white wine like Sauvignon Blanc.
- Complement Barbecue Potato Chips with a bold and fruity red wine such as Zinfandel.
- Match Sour Cream and Onion Potato Chips with a creamy Chardonnay.

Gourmet Potato Chips:

- Pair Truffle Oil and Parmesan Potato Chips with a sparkling Prosecco.
- Enjoy Rosemary and Sea Salt Potato Chips with a hoppy IPA or a citrusy pale ale.
- Accompany Sriracha Lime Potato Chips with a refreshing margarita.

C. Appetizer Platter Ideas
Classic Potato Chips:

- Create a classic chip and dip platter with a variety of dips.
- Combine with cheese and charcuterie for a simple yet satisfying spread.

Flavored Potato Chips:

- Arrange on a platter with corresponding dips for a flavor-packed snack.
- Pair with cheese and fruit for a gourmet appetizer board.

Gourmet Potato Chips:

- Showcase the chips alongside gourmet cheeses, olives, and cured meats.
- Create a Mediterranean-inspired platter with hummus, tzatziki, and marinated vegetables.

D. Dessert Combinations

Chocolate Covered Potato Chips:

- Serve alongside a scoop of vanilla ice cream for a sweet and salty dessert.
- Dip half of the chocolate-covered chips in crushed nuts for added texture.

Sweet Potato Chips:

- Pair with a creamy cinnamon yogurt dip for a light and satisfying dessert option.
- Serve alongside a fruit salsa made with diced mango, pineapple, and kiwi.

Trail Mix with Potato Chips:

- Incorporate into homemade granola bars or cookies for a crunchy surprise.
- Sprinkle over vanilla or chocolate pudding for a crunchy topping.

These serving suggestions and pairings will enhance the enjoyment of your potato chip creations and make them the highlight of any gathering or snack time.

Chapter (8) Troubleshooting and FAQs

A. Common Problems and Solutions

1. Soggy Chips: If your chips turn out soggy, it's likely due to excess moisture in the potatoes. Ensure you thoroughly dry the potato slices before frying. Additionally, frying at the correct temperature (around 350°F or 175°C) and not overcrowding the frying vessel can help prevent soggy chips.
2. Burnt Chips: Burning can occur if the oil temperature is too high or if the chips are left in the oil for too long. Monitor the oil temperature closely with a thermometer and adjust the heat as needed. Remove the chips from the oil when they are golden brown and crispy.
3. Unevenly Cooked Chips: Unevenly cooked chips may result from inconsistent slicing thickness. Use a mandoline slicer or knife to ensure uniform slices. Additionally, fry the chips in batches to ensure even cooking.
4. Salty Chips: If your chips turn out too salty, reduce the amount of salt you sprinkle over them after frying. You can also try using low-sodium varieties of seasonings or omitting additional salt altogether.

B. Storage and Shelf Life

1. Room Temperature: Allow homemade potato chips to cool completely before storing them in an airtight container at room temperature. They will remain crispy for up to 2-3 days.
2. Refrigeration: While refrigeration is not necessary, storing potato chips in the refrigerator can help prolong their shelf life. Place them in an airtight container or resealable plastic bag and store in the refrigerator for up to 1 week.

3. Freezing: Potato chips can be frozen for longer-term storage. Place them in a single layer on a baking sheet and freeze until solid, then transfer to a freezer-safe container or bag. Frozen potato chips can be stored for up to 2 months. Thaw at room temperature before reheating in the oven to restore crispiness.

C. Frequently Asked Questions

1. Can I reuse the frying oil?: Yes, you can reuse frying oil for making potato chips multiple times. Allow the oil to cool completely, then strain it through a fine-mesh sieve or cheesecloth to remove any debris. Store the strained oil in a cool, dark place and use it within a few weeks for best results.
2. Can I use different types of potatoes for making chips?: While Russet and Yukon Gold potatoes are commonly used for making potato chips due to their low moisture content and high starch content, you can experiment with other varieties as well. Just keep in mind that the texture and flavor may vary depending on the type of potato used.
3. How can I make healthier potato chips?: To make healthier potato chips, consider baking or air frying them instead of deep frying. You can also use sweet potatoes or other vegetables as an alternative to regular potatoes. Additionally, season the chips with herbs and spices instead of salt for a lower sodium option.
4. Can I make potato chips ahead of time for a party?: Yes, you can make potato chips ahead of time for a party. Store them in an airtight container at room temperature or in the refrigerator until ready to serve. If needed, you can reheat them in the oven briefly to restore crispiness before serving.

These troubleshooting tips and FAQs will help you overcome common challenges and ensure your homemade potato chips turn out perfectly every time.

Chapter (9) Potato Chip Inspired Side Dishes

A. Potato Chip Crusted Fish Fillets
  Ingredients:

- Fish fillets (such as cod, tilapia, or salmon)
- Potato chips, crushed
- All-purpose flour
- Eggs, beaten
- Salt and pepper, to taste
- Olive oil or cooking spray

Instructions:

1. Preheat the oven to 400°F (200°C). Line a baking sheet with parchment paper.
2. Season the fish fillets with salt and pepper.
3. Dredge each fish fillet in flour, then dip into beaten eggs, and finally coat with crushed potato chips.
4. Place the coated fish fillets on the prepared baking sheet.
5. Drizzle olive oil over the fish fillets or spray with cooking spray.
6. Bake in the preheated oven for 15-20 minutes, or until the fish is cooked through and the potato chip crust is golden brown and crispy.
7. Serve the potato chip crusted fish fillets hot with lemon wedges and tartar sauce.

B. Potato Chip Crusted Mac and Cheese
  Ingredients:

- Cooked macaroni pasta
- Cheese sauce (homemade or store-bought)
- Potato chips, crushed
- Butter, melted
- Optional: additional shredded cheese for topping

Instructions:

1. Preheat the oven to 375°F (190°C). Grease a baking dish with butter or cooking spray.
2. In a large mixing bowl, combine the cooked macaroni pasta and cheese sauce until well coated.
3. Transfer the mac and cheese mixture to the prepared baking dish.
4. Sprinkle crushed potato chips evenly over the top of the mac and cheese.
5. Drizzle melted butter over the potato chip layer.
6. If desired, sprinkle additional shredded cheese over the top for extra cheesiness.
7. Bake in the preheated oven for 20-25 minutes, or until the cheese is bubbly and the potato chip crust is golden brown and crispy.
8. Serve the potato chip crusted mac and cheese hot as a delicious and comforting side dish.

C. Loaded Potato Chip Nachos
Ingredients:

- Potato chips (thick-cut or kettle-cooked work best)
- Shredded cheese (cheddar, Monterey Jack, or a blend)
- Cooked and seasoned ground beef or turkey
- Black beans, drained and rinsed
- Diced tomatoes

- Sliced jalapeños
- Sliced black olives
- Chopped green onions
- Sour cream
- Guacamole or diced avocado
- Salsa
- Optional toppings: sliced red onions, diced bell peppers, cooked corn kernels, chopped cilantro

Instructions:

1. Preheat the oven to 375°F (190°C).
2. Spread a layer of potato chips on a large baking sheet lined with parchment paper or aluminum foil.
3. Sprinkle a generous amount of shredded cheese over the potato chips.
4. Top the cheese with cooked and seasoned ground beef or turkey, black beans, diced tomatoes, sliced jalapeños, and black olives.
5. Place the baking sheet in the preheated oven and bake for 8-10 minutes, or until the cheese is melted and bubbly.
6. Remove from the oven and garnish the loaded potato chip nachos with chopped green onions.
7. Serve immediately with sour cream, guacamole or diced avocado, and salsa on the side.
8. Optional: Add any additional toppings of your choice before serving.
9. Enjoy the crispy, cheesy, and flavorful loaded potato chip nachos as a delicious appetizer or snack!

D. Potato Chip Crusted Veggie Casserole
Ingredients:

- 4 cups mixed vegetables (such as broccoli, cauliflower, carrots, and peas), cooked
- 1 cup shredded cheese (cheddar, mozzarella, or your favorite blend)
- 1 cup milk
- 2 tablespoons all-purpose flour
- 2 tablespoons butter
- 1 cup potato chips, crushed
- Salt and pepper, to taste

Instructions:

1. Preheat the oven to 375°F (190°C). Grease a baking dish with butter or cooking spray.
2. Spread the cooked mixed vegetables evenly in the prepared baking dish.
3. In a saucepan over medium heat, melt the butter. Whisk in the flour to form a roux, cooking for 1-2 minutes until golden brown.
4. Gradually whisk in the milk, stirring constantly until the sauce thickens and becomes smooth.
5. Remove the saucepan from heat and stir in the shredded cheese until melted and well combined. Season with salt and pepper to taste.
6. Pour the cheese sauce over the mixed vegetables in the baking dish, ensuring they are evenly coated.
7. Sprinkle the crushed potato chips evenly over the top of the casserole.
8. Bake in the preheated oven for 20-25 minutes, or until the cheese is bubbly and the potato chip crust is golden brown and crispy.
9. Remove from the oven and let it cool for a few minutes before serving.

10. Serve the potato chip crusted veggie casserole as a flavorful and satisfying side dish alongside your favorite main course. Enjoy the crispy topping and creamy vegetable filling!

E. Potato Chip Encrusted Baked Potatoes
Ingredients:

- 4 large russet potatoes
- Olive oil
- Salt and pepper, to taste
- 1 cup potato chips, crushed
- Sour cream, for serving
- Chopped chives or green onions, for garnish

Instructions:

1. Preheat the oven to 400°F (200°C).
2. Scrub the potatoes clean and dry them thoroughly with a paper towel.
3. Pierce each potato several times with a fork to allow steam to escape during baking.
4. Rub the potatoes with olive oil and sprinkle with salt and pepper.
5. Roll each potato in the crushed potato chips, pressing gently to adhere the chips to the surface.
6. Place the coated potatoes directly on the oven rack or on a baking sheet lined with aluminum foil.
7. Bake for 45-60 minutes, or until the potatoes are tender when pierced with a fork and the potato chip crust is golden brown and crispy.
8. Remove the baked potatoes from the oven and let them cool for a few minutes.
9. Slice each potato lengthwise and fluff the insides with a fork.

10. Serve the potato chip encrusted baked potatoes hot, topped with sour cream and chopped chives or green onions.

11. Enjoy these crunchy and flavorful baked potatoes as a delicious side dish or a satisfying main course!

Chapter (10) Seasonal Potato Chip Specialties

A. Pumpkin Spice Potato Chips (Fall)
Ingredients:

- 2 large sweet potatoes, thinly sliced
- Vegetable oil for frying
- Pumpkin spice mix (cinnamon, nutmeg, ginger, cloves)
- Granulated sugar

Instructions:

1. Follow the same instructions as for making sweet potato chips.
2. While the chips are still hot, sprinkle them generously with the pumpkin spice mix and granulated sugar.
3. Toss gently to ensure the spices and sugar coat the chips evenly.
4. Allow the pumpkin spice sweet potato chips to cool before serving. Enjoy the warm and comforting flavors of fall in every crunchy bite!

B. Cranberry and Brie Potato Chips (Winter)
Ingredients:

- 2 large russet potatoes, thinly sliced
- Vegetable oil for frying
- Dried cranberries, chopped
- Brie cheese, thinly sliced
- Fresh rosemary, chopped
- Salt, to taste

Instructions:

1. Follow the same instructions as for making classic potato chips.
2. While the chips are still hot, top them with thinly sliced Brie cheese.
3. Sprinkle chopped dried cranberries and fresh rosemary over the Brie cheese.
4. Season with salt to taste.
5. Allow the cranberry and Brie potato chips to cool slightly before serving. Enjoy the festive and indulgent flavors of winter!

C. Zesty Lemon Pepper Potato Chips (Spring)
Ingredients:

- 2 large russet potatoes, thinly sliced
- Vegetable oil for frying
- Lemon zest
- Black pepper
- Fresh parsley, chopped
- Salt, to taste

Instructions:

1. Follow the same instructions as for making classic potato chips.
2. While the chips are still hot, sprinkle them generously with lemon zest and freshly ground black pepper.
3. Garnish with chopped fresh parsley and season with salt to taste.
4. Allow the zesty lemon pepper potato chips to cool before serving. Enjoy the bright and refreshing flavors of spring!

D. BBQ Ranch Potato Chips (Summer)
Ingredients:

- 2 large russet potatoes, thinly sliced
- Vegetable oil for frying
- BBQ seasoning or sauce
- Ranch seasoning mix
- Salt, to taste

Instructions:

1. Follow the same instructions as for making classic potato chips.
2. While the chips are still hot, sprinkle them generously with BBQ seasoning or drizzle with BBQ sauce.
3. Sprinkle ranch seasoning mix over the BBQ-coated chips.
4. Season with salt to taste.
5. Allow the BBQ ranch potato chips to cool before serving. Enjoy the smoky, tangy, and creamy flavors reminiscent of summer BBQs!

E. Cinnamon Sugar Sweet Potato Chips (Anytime)
Ingredients:

- 2 large sweet potatoes, thinly sliced
- Vegetable oil for frying
- Ground cinnamon
- Granulated sugar

Instructions:

1. Follow the same instructions as for making sweet potato chips.
2. While the chips are still hot, sprinkle them generously with ground cinnamon and granulated sugar.
3. Toss gently to ensure the cinnamon sugar coats the chips evenly.
4. Allow the cinnamon sugar sweet potato chips to cool before serving. Enjoy the irresistible combination of sweet and spicy flavors any time of the year!

Chapter (11) Potato Chip Pairings for Entertaining

A. Wine and Potato Chip Pairing Guide

1. Classic Potato Chips: Pair with a dry sparkling wine like Champagne or Prosecco. The effervescence helps cut through the saltiness of the chips.
2. Barbecue Potato Chips: Match with a bold and fruity red wine such as Zinfandel or Syrah. The smoky flavors of the BBQ chips complement the richness of these wines.
3. Sour Cream and Onion Potato Chips: Enjoy with a crisp and refreshing white wine like Sauvignon Blanc or Pinot Grigio. The acidity of the wine balances the creamy onion flavors.
4. Truffle Oil and Parmesan Potato Chips: Pair with a luxurious Champagne or a dry white wine like Chardonnay. The earthy truffle notes and savory Parmesan cheese are enhanced by these wines.

B. Cheese and Charcuterie Board with Potato Chips

Create a beautiful spread featuring an assortment of cheeses, cured meats, fruits, nuts, and of course, potato chips! Arrange the potato chips on the board alongside the other elements, offering guests a crunchy and flavorful addition to the cheese and charcuterie experience.

C. Potato Chip Flight Tasting Party

Host a tasting party where guests can sample a variety of potato chip flavors from classic to gourmet. Provide tasting notes and encourage guests to discuss their favorite flavors and pairings. Consider offering small bites such as cheese, crackers, and fresh fruit to cleanse the palate between chip tastings.

D. Potato Chip Inspired Cocktail Hour

Craft cocktails inspired by the flavors of different potato chip varieties. For example:

1. Create a BBQ Ranch Martini using BBQ-infused vodka and a splash of ranch dressing.
2. Mix up a Truffle Sour with bourbon, lemon juice, simple syrup, and a splash of truffle oil.
3. Shake up a Sour Cream and Onion Gin Fizz with gin, sour cream, onion-infused syrup, and club soda.
4. Serve these inventive cocktails alongside a selection of potato chips for a fun and flavorful cocktail hour experience. Encourage guests to experiment with different chip and cocktail pairings to find their perfect match!

Chapter (12) Potato Chip Preservation and Packaging

A. Tips for Preserving Freshness

1. Air-Tight Containers: Transfer potato chips to air-tight containers or resealable bags to help maintain their freshness and crispiness.
2. Avoid Moisture: Keep potato chips away from moisture, as it can cause them to become soggy. Store them in a cool, dry place.
3. Use Silica Gel Packs: Place silica gel packs in the container with the potato chips to help absorb any excess moisture and keep them fresh longer.
4. Re-Seal Bags: If you're not using a container, ensure that you tightly reseal the original packaging after opening to prevent air and moisture from getting in.

B. Packaging Ideas for Gifting

1. Decorative Tins: Package potato chips in decorative tins or boxes for an elegant and festive presentation.
2. Mason Jars: Layer potato chips in mason jars and tie a ribbon or twine around the lid for a rustic and charming look.
3. Cellophane Bags: Place potato chips in cellophane bags and tie them with colorful ribbon or string for a simple yet attractive packaging option.
4. Personalized Labels: Create personalized labels or tags to attach to the packaging, adding a special touch for gift-giving occasions.

C. Creative Storage Solutions for Bulk Batches

1. Vacuum Sealer: Use a vacuum sealer to portion and vacuum seal bulk batches of potato chips, extending their shelf life and maintaining freshness.
2. Large Airtight Containers: Invest in large airtight containers or storage bins specifically designed for storing bulk quantities of snacks like potato chips.
3. Divided Storage Bins: Use divided storage bins or organizers to separate different flavors or varieties of potato chips, making it easy to access and rotate your snack inventory.
4. Pantry Storage: Allocate a dedicated section of your pantry or cupboard for storing bulk batches of potato chips, keeping them organized and easily accessible for snacking or gifting.

D. Making and Storing Flavored Salts for Seasoning

1. Flavored Salt Varieties: Experiment with different flavored salts to enhance the taste of your potato chips, such as garlic salt, onion salt, or smoked salt.
2. Homemade Flavored Salts: Make your own flavored salts by mixing sea salt with dried herbs, spices, or citrus zest. Store them in airtight containers for future use.
3. Storage Containers: Transfer homemade flavored salts to small jars or containers with tight-fitting lids to keep them fresh and flavorful.
4. Labeling: Label each container with the type of flavored salt and the date it was made to ensure you use them before they lose their potency.

By following these preservation and packaging tips, you can ensure your potato chips stay fresh and flavorful, whether you're storing them for personal enjoyment or preparing them as gifts for friends and family.

Chapter (13) Potato Chip Artistry and Presentation

A. Techniques for Creative Slicing and Shapes

1. Mandoline Slicer: Use a mandoline slicer to create uniform potato slices of varying thickness. Experiment with different settings to achieve thin, crispy chips or thicker, heartier slices.
2. Wavy Cutter: Try using a wavy cutter or crinkle cutter to add texture and visual interest to your potato chips.
3. Vegetable Peeler: Use a vegetable peeler to create ribbon-like potato slices for a unique presentation.
4. Cookie Cutters: Use cookie cutters to cut out potato slices in fun shapes like stars, hearts, or animals for a playful twist.

B. Garnishing and Plating Strategies

1. Layering: Arrange potato chips in overlapping layers on a serving platter to create a visually appealing presentation.
2. Height Variation: Create height variation by stacking potato chips in a pyramid or arranging them in a spiral pattern on the plate.
3. Color Contrast: Pair light-colored potato chips with dark-colored dips or sauces for contrast, or sprinkle colorful garnishes like chopped herbs or edible flowers over the chips for a pop of color.
4. Serve in Unique Containers: Serve potato chips in unconventional containers such as mini baskets, parchment paper cones, or hollowed-out vegetables for a creative presentation.

C. Using Potato Chips as Edible Decorations

1. Crushed Toppings: Use crushed potato chips as a crunchy topping for salads, soups, or baked dishes for added texture and flavor.
2. Edible Bowls: Mold softened potato chips into edible bowls or cups using muffin tins or small bowls as molds. Fill them with dips, salads, or even ice cream for a playful presentation.
3. Garnish and Accents: Use whole or halved potato chips as garnishes or accents on plated dishes to add a whimsical touch and hint at the flavor profile of the dish.

D. Hosting a Potato Chip Decorating Party

1. Provide a Variety of Ingredients: Set up a spread with different types of potato chips, dips, sauces, and toppings for guests to experiment with.
2. Creative Stations: Create stations with themed toppings such as sweet, savory, spicy, and tangy to inspire guests' creativity.
3. DIY Potato Chip Bar: Set up a DIY potato chip bar where guests can assemble their own custom chip creations using a variety of ingredients and flavor combinations.
4. Friendly Competition: Turn the decorating party into a friendly competition by having guests vote on their favorite chip creations. Offer small prizes for the most creative, flavorful, or visually stunning chips.

By incorporating these techniques and hosting a potato chip decorating party, you can elevate the artistry and presentation of potato chips, turning them into a fun and interactive culinary experience for yourself and your guests.

Chapter (14) Potato Chip Dessert Innovations

A. Potato Chip Chocolate Chunk Cookies
Ingredients:

- 1 cup unsalted butter, softened
- 1 cup granulated sugar
- 1 cup brown sugar
- 2 large eggs
- 1 teaspoon vanilla extract
- 2 cups all-purpose flour
- 1 teaspoon baking soda
- 1/2 teaspoon salt
- 2 cups potato chips, crushed
- 1 cup chocolate chunks or chips

Instructions:

1. Preheat the oven to 350°F (175°C). Line baking sheets with parchment paper.
2. In a large mixing bowl, cream together the softened butter, granulated sugar, and brown sugar until light and fluffy.
3. Beat in the eggs one at a time, then stir in the vanilla extract.
4. In a separate bowl, whisk together the flour, baking soda, and salt. Gradually add the dry ingredients to the wet ingredients, mixing until just combined.
5. Fold in the crushed potato chips and chocolate chunks until evenly distributed throughout the dough.
6. Drop rounded tablespoons of dough onto the prepared baking sheets, spacing them about 2 inches apart.
7. Bake in the preheated oven for 10-12 minutes, or until the edges

are golden brown.

8. Allow the cookies to cool on the baking sheets for a few minutes before transferring them to wire racks to cool completely. Enjoy the sweet and salty goodness of potato chip chocolate chunk cookies!

B. Potato Chip Blondies
Ingredients:

- 1 cup unsalted butter, melted
- 1 cup brown sugar
- 1/2 cup granulated sugar
- 2 large eggs
- 1 teaspoon vanilla extract
- 2 cups all-purpose flour
- 1 teaspoon baking powder
- 1/2 teaspoon salt
- 1 1/2 cups potato chips, crushed
- 1 cup white chocolate chips

Instructions:

1. Preheat the oven to 350°F (175°C). Grease a 9x13-inch baking dish.
2. In a large mixing bowl, whisk together the melted butter, brown sugar, and granulated sugar until well combined.
3. Beat in the eggs one at a time, then stir in the vanilla extract.
4. In a separate bowl, sift together the flour, baking powder, and salt. Gradually add the dry ingredients to the wet ingredients, mixing until just combined.
5. Fold in the crushed potato chips and white chocolate chips until evenly distributed throughout the batter.
6. Spread the batter evenly into the prepared baking dish.

7. Bake in the preheated oven for 25-30 minutes, or until the top is golden brown and a toothpick inserted into the center comes out clean.

8. Allow the blondies to cool in the baking dish before slicing and serving. Enjoy the chewy texture and salty-sweet flavor of potato chip blondies!

C. Potato Chip Crusted Cheesecake
Ingredients:

- 2 cups potato chips, crushed
- 1/4 cup unsalted butter, melted
- 24 oz cream cheese, softened
- 3/4 cup granulated sugar
- 3 large eggs
- 1 teaspoon vanilla extract
- 1 cup sour cream
- 1/4 cup all-purpose flour
- Optional: additional potato chips for garnish

Instructions:

1. Preheat the oven to 325°F (160°C). Grease a 9-inch springform pan.

2. In a mixing bowl, combine the crushed potato chips and melted butter. Press the mixture evenly into the bottom of the prepared springform pan to form the crust.

3. In a large mixing bowl, beat the softened cream cheese and sugar until smooth and creamy.

4. Add the eggs one at a time, beating well after each addition. Mix in the vanilla extract.

5. Stir in the sour cream and flour until well combined and smooth.

6. Pour the cheesecake batter over the potato chip crust in the springform pan.
7. Bake in the preheated oven for 45-50 minutes, or until the edges are set and the center is slightly jiggly.
8. Turn off the oven and leave the cheesecake inside with the door slightly ajar for 1 hour to cool gradually.
9. Remove the cheesecake from the oven and let it cool completely at room temperature.
10. Once cooled, refrigerate the cheesecake for at least 4 hours or overnight to set.
11. Before serving, garnish with additional crushed potato chips if desired.
12. Slice and serve the potato chip crusted cheesecake for a unique and delicious dessert!

D. Potato Chip Ice Cream Sundae
Ingredients:

- Vanilla ice cream
- Chocolate syrup or hot fudge
- Caramel sauce
- Whipped cream
- Maraschino cherries
- Potato chips, crushed
- Optional: sprinkles or chopped nuts for garnish

Instructions:

1. Scoop vanilla ice cream into serving bowls or dishes.
2. Drizzle chocolate syrup or hot fudge and caramel sauce over the ice cream.
3. Top with whipped cream and a maraschino cherry.
4. Sprinkle crushed potato chips over the top of the sundae.

5. Optional: Add sprinkles or chopped nuts for extra flavor and texture.
6. Serve immediately and enjoy the sweet and salty combination of flavors in this indulgent potato chip ice cream sundae!

E. Potato Chip Rice Krispie Treats
Ingredients:

- 6 cups crispy rice cereal
- 4 cups mini marshmallows
- 3 tablespoons unsalted butter
- 2 cups potato chips, crushed
- Optional: chocolate chips or drizzle for garnish

Instructions:

1. In a large pot, melt the butter over low heat.
2. Add the mini marshmallows to the melted butter, stirring constantly until completely melted and smooth.
3. Remove the pot from heat and quickly stir in the crispy rice cereal until evenly coated with the marshmallow mixture.
4. Gently fold in the crushed potato chips until well distributed throughout the mixture.
5. Press the mixture evenly into a greased 9x13-inch baking dish using a spatula or wax paper.
6. If desired, sprinkle chocolate chips over the top of the mixture or drizzle with melted chocolate for added sweetness.
7. Allow the treats to cool and set at room temperature for about 1 hour before cutting into squares.
8. Serve and enjoy the unique and crunchy texture of potato chip rice krispie treats as a fun and tasty dessert or snack!

Chapter (15) Potato Chip Fusion Cuisine

A. Kimchi Potato Chip Tacos (Korean-Mexican Fusion)
Ingredients:

- Soft corn or flour tortillas
- Kimchi
- Cooked shredded chicken or beef bulgogi
- Potato chips
- Sriracha mayo or gochujang mayo
- Chopped green onions
- Sesame seeds (optional)

Instructions:

1. Warm the tortillas in a skillet or microwave until soft and pliable.
2. Layer kimchi and cooked shredded chicken or beef bulgogi on the tortillas.
3. Crush potato chips and sprinkle them over the filling.
4. Drizzle with sriracha mayo or gochujang mayo.
5. Garnish with chopped green onions and sesame seeds, if desired.
6. Fold the tortillas and serve immediately for a delicious fusion of Korean and Mexican flavors.

B. Teriyaki Chicken and Pineapple Potato Chip Bowls (Japanese-Hawaiian Fusion)
Ingredients:

- Cooked white rice
- Teriyaki chicken (grilled or stir-fried)
- Pineapple chunks

- Potato chips
- Teriyaki sauce
- Green onions, chopped
- Sesame seeds

Instructions:

1. Place cooked white rice in serving bowls.
2. Top with teriyaki chicken and pineapple chunks.
3. Crush potato chips and sprinkle them over the bowls.
4. Drizzle with teriyaki sauce.
5. Garnish with chopped green onions and sesame seeds.
6. Serve immediately for a fusion of Japanese and Hawaiian flavors with a crunchy twist.

C. Curry Chicken Potato Chip Wraps (Indian-British Fusion)
Ingredients:

- Tortilla wraps or naan bread
- Curry chicken (cooked chicken in curry sauce)
- Potato chips
- Mango chutney or yogurt sauce
- Fresh cilantro leaves
- Sliced cucumbers (optional)

Instructions:

1. Warm tortilla wraps or naan bread.
2. Spread a layer of curry chicken onto each wrap or naan.
3. Crush potato chips and sprinkle them over the curry chicken.
4. Drizzle with mango chutney or yogurt sauce.
5. Top with fresh cilantro leaves and sliced cucumbers, if desired.
6. Roll up the wraps or fold the naan and serve immediately for a flavorful fusion of Indian and British cuisines.

D. Poutine with Gravy and Cheese Curds Topped with Potato Chips (Canadian-American Fusion)

Ingredients:

- French fries
- Cheese curds
- Gravy
- Potato chips
- Chopped green onions (optional)

Instructions:

1. Prepare French fries according to your preferred method.
2. Place the cooked fries on a serving platter or in individual bowls.
3. Sprinkle cheese curds over the fries.
4. Pour hot gravy over the fries and cheese curds.
5. Crush potato chips and sprinkle them over the poutine.
6. Garnish with chopped green onions, if desired.
7. Serve immediately for a delicious fusion of Canadian and American flavors with an added crunch.

E. Mediterranean Potato Chip Salad with Feta and Olives (Mediterranean-American Fusion)

Ingredients:

- Mixed greens (such as lettuce, spinach, or arugula)
- Cherry tomatoes, halved
- Cucumber, sliced
- Red onion, thinly sliced
- Feta cheese, crumbled
- Kalamata olives, pitted

- Potato chips
- Greek dressing or balsamic vinaigrette

Instructions:

1. In a large salad bowl, combine mixed greens, cherry tomatoes, cucumber slices, red onion slices, crumbled feta cheese, and Kalamata olives.
2. Crush potato chips and sprinkle them over the salad.
3. Drizzle with Greek dressing or balsamic vinaigrette.
4. Toss gently to coat all ingredients with the dressing.
5. Serve immediately for a refreshing fusion of Mediterranean and American flavors with a crispy twist.

Chapter (16) Potato Chip Cocktails and Mocktails

A. Spicy Bloody Mary with Potato Chip Garnish
Ingredients:

- 1 1/2 oz vodka
- 3 oz tomato juice
- 1/2 oz lemon juice
- 1/4 tsp Worcestershire sauce
- 1/4 tsp hot sauce (adjust to taste)
- Pinch of salt and pepper
- Celery salt, for rimming
- Potato chips, for garnish
- Celery stalk, for garnish
- Lemon wedge, for garnish

Instructions:

1. Rim a glass with celery salt by running a lemon wedge around the rim and dipping it in celery salt.
2. Fill the glass with ice cubes.
3. In a shaker, combine vodka, tomato juice, lemon juice, Worcestershire sauce, hot sauce, salt, and pepper. Shake well.
4. Strain the mixture into the prepared glass.
5. Garnish with a stalk of celery, a lemon wedge, and a few potato chips. Serve immediately.

B. Potato Chip Martini
Ingredients:

- 2 oz potato chip-infused vodka (see instructions below)
- 1/2 oz dry vermouth

- Potato chips, for garnish

Instructions:

1. To make potato chip-infused vodka, crush a handful of potato chips and add them to a jar with vodka. Let it infuse for at least 24 hours, then strain out the potato chips.
2. Fill a mixing glass with ice cubes.
3. Add the potato chip-infused vodka and dry vermouth. Stir well.
4. Strain the mixture into a chilled martini glass.
5. Garnish with a potato chip. Serve immediately.

C. Pineapple Potato Chip Mojito (Mocktail)
Ingredients:

- 1/2 cup pineapple juice
- 1/4 cup coconut water
- 6-8 fresh mint leaves
- 1/2 lime, juiced
- Soda water
- Potato chips, for garnish

Instructions:

1. In a glass, muddle fresh mint leaves with lime juice.
2. Add pineapple juice and coconut water. Stir well.
3. Fill the glass with ice cubes.
4. Top up with soda water and stir gently.
5. Garnish with a sprig of mint and a few potato chips. Serve immediately.

D. Potato Chip-infused Vodka Lemonade
Ingredients:

- 2 oz potato chip-infused vodka
- 4 oz lemonade
- Ice cubes
- Lemon slice, for garnish
- Potato chips, for garnish

Instructions:

1. Fill a glass with ice cubes.
2. Add potato chip-infused vodka and lemonade. Stir well.
3. Garnish with a slice of lemon and a few potato chips. Serve immediately.

E. Sparkling Potato Chip Punch (Mocktail)
Ingredients:

- 2 cups sparkling water
- 1/2 cup pineapple juice
- 1/4 cup orange juice
- 1/4 cup cranberry juice
- Potato chips, for garnish

Instructions:

1. In a pitcher, combine sparkling water, pineapple juice, orange juice, and cranberry juice. Stir well.
2. Fill glasses with ice cubes.
3. Pour the sparkling punch into the glasses.
4. Garnish with a few potato chips. Serve immediately.

Chapter (17) Potato Chip Brunch Extravaganza

A. Potato Chip Breakfast Casserole
Ingredients:

- 6 cups frozen shredded hash browns, thawed
- 1 cup cooked and crumbled breakfast sausage
- 1 cup shredded cheddar cheese
- 1 cup sour cream
- 1 can condensed cream of mushroom soup
- 1/2 cup diced onion
- 1/2 cup diced bell pepper
- 1/4 teaspoon garlic powder
- Salt and pepper, to taste
- 2 cups potato chips, crushed
- Optional: chopped green onions for garnish

Instructions:

1. Preheat the oven to 350°F (175°C). Grease a 9x13-inch baking dish.
2. In a large mixing bowl, combine thawed hash browns, cooked breakfast sausage, shredded cheddar cheese, sour cream, condensed cream of mushroom soup, diced onion, diced bell pepper, garlic powder, salt, and pepper. Mix until well combined.
3. Spread the mixture evenly into the prepared baking dish.
4. Sprinkle crushed potato chips over the top of the casserole.
5. Cover the baking dish with aluminum foil and bake in the preheated oven for 45 minutes.
6. Remove the foil and continue baking for an additional 15

minutes, or until the casserole is hot and bubbly, and the potato chips are golden brown.

7. Let the casserole cool for a few minutes before serving. Garnish with chopped green onions if desired.

B. Potato Chip Pancakes with Maple Syrup
Ingredients:

- Prepared pancake batter
- Potato chips, crushed
- Maple syrup
- Butter

Instructions:

1. Prepare pancake batter according to your favorite recipe or package instructions.
2. Fold crushed potato chips into the pancake batter.
3. Heat a griddle or non-stick skillet over medium heat and lightly grease with butter.
4. Pour batter onto the griddle to form pancakes of desired size.
5. Cook until bubbles form on the surface of the pancakes, then flip and cook until golden brown on the other side.
6. Serve the potato chip pancakes warm with maple syrup drizzled on top.

C. Eggs Benedict with Potato Chip Hollandaise Sauce
Ingredients:

- English muffins, split and toasted
- Canadian bacon or ham slices, cooked
- Poached eggs

- Potato chip hollandaise sauce (see instructions below)
- Chopped chives, for garnish

Potato Chip Hollandaise Sauce:

- 3 egg yolks
- 1 tablespoon lemon juice
- 1/2 cup unsalted butter, melted
- 1/4 cup crushed potato chips
- Salt and pepper, to taste

Instructions for Potato Chip Hollandaise Sauce:

1. In a blender or food processor, combine egg yolks and lemon juice. Blend until smooth.
2. While blending, slowly pour in the melted butter in a steady stream until the sauce thickens.
3. Stir in crushed potato chips and season with salt and pepper to taste. Keep warm until ready to use.

Assembly:

1. Place toasted English muffin halves on serving plates.
2. Top each muffin half with a slice of Canadian bacon or ham.
3. Carefully place a poached egg on top of each slice of bacon.
4. Spoon potato chip hollandaise sauce generously over the eggs.
5. Garnish with chopped chives and serve immediately.

D. Breakfast Burritos with Crumbled Potato Chips
Ingredients:

- Large flour tortillas
- Scrambled eggs
- Cooked breakfast sausage or bacon

- Shredded cheddar cheese
- Diced tomatoes
- Diced green onions
- Sour cream
- Salsa
- Crushed potato chips

Instructions:

1. Lay out a tortilla on a flat surface.
2. Fill the center of the tortilla with scrambled eggs, cooked breakfast sausage or bacon, shredded cheddar cheese, diced tomatoes, diced green onions, sour cream, salsa, and crushed potato chips.
3. Fold in the sides of the tortilla, then roll it up tightly to form a burrito.
4. Place the burrito seam-side down on a heated skillet or griddle.
5. Cook the burrito until golden brown and crispy on all sides.
6. Serve the breakfast burrito warm, garnished with extra crushed potato chips on top.

E. Potato Chip Breakfast Sandwiches
  Ingredients:

- English muffins or bagels, split and toasted
- Fried or scrambled eggs
- Cooked bacon or sausage patties
- Sliced cheese (such as cheddar or American)
- Potato chips
- Optional: sliced avocado, tomato slices, lettuce

Instructions:

1. Place a cooked egg, bacon or sausage patty, and a slice of cheese on the bottom half of each English muffin or bagel.
2. Top with a handful of potato chips for crunch.
3. Add any optional toppings such as sliced avocado, tomato slices, or lettuce.
4. Place the top half of the English muffin or bagel over the fillings to form a sandwich.
5. Serve the potato chip breakfast sandwiches immediately, and enjoy the satisfying combination of flavors and textures.

Chapter (18) Potato Chip Cooking Challenges

A. Potato Chip Mystery Box Challenge

In this challenge, contestants are given a mystery box containing a variety of ingredients along with a large quantity of potato chips. They have a limited amount of time to create a dish using the provided ingredients, with potato chips being a required element. The challenge tests creativity, resourcefulness, and the ability to adapt to unexpected ingredients.

B. Potato Chip Speed Cooking Competition

Contestants compete head-to-head in a timed cooking competition where they must incorporate potato chips into their dishes. They have a limited amount of time, such as 30 minutes or an hour, to prepare and present their creations to the judges. The emphasis is on speed, efficiency, and the ability to think on their feet while utilizing the unique texture and flavor of potato chips.

C. Potato Chip Cooking Relay Race

Teams of contestants participate in a relay race-style cooking competition where each member takes turns preparing a dish using potato chips as a key ingredient. The relay format adds an element of teamwork and coordination as teammates must communicate effectively to complete each stage of the cooking process. The team that finishes all stages of the relay and presents the most impressive final dish wins the competition.

D. Potato Chip Iron Chef Battle

Inspired by the popular television show "Iron Chef," this challenge pits two talented chefs against each other in a culinary showdown featuring potato chips as the secret ingredient. The chefs have a set amount of time, typically 60 minutes, to create multiple dishes showcasing the versatility of potato chips. A panel of judges evaluates each chef's creations based on taste, creativity, presentation, and effective use of the secret ingredient.

E. Potato Chip Recipe Swap Challenge

In this challenge, contestants exchange their signature potato chip recipes with each other and must recreate and present the dishes as accurately as possible. Each contestant receives a recipe from another participant and has to follow it closely while adding their own unique twist. This challenge encourages creativity, adaptability, and the ability to execute recipes from different culinary styles and backgrounds.

❖ Conclusion

A. Final tips for perfecting potato chip recipes:

- Use high-quality potatoes and slice them uniformly for consistent cooking.
- Monitor oil temperature closely when frying potato chips to achieve the perfect crispiness.
- Season chips immediately after frying while they're still hot to ensure the seasoning adheres well.
- Experiment with different flavor combinations and seasoning blends to create unique and delicious potato chip recipes.
- Don't be afraid to adjust cooking times and temperatures based on your preferences and equipment.

B. Encouragement to experiment and enjoy the process:

- Cooking with potato chips is all about creativity and innovation, so don't hesitate to think outside the box and try new ideas.
- Embrace the joy of cooking and have fun experimenting with different flavors, textures, and presentations.
- Remember that mistakes are part of the learning process, so don't be discouraged if a recipe doesn't turn out perfectly the first time.
- Take pride in your creations and enjoy the satisfaction of sharing delicious homemade potato chips with friends and family.

C. Invitation to share creations and feedback:

- We'd love to see your potato chip creations! Share photos of your recipes and experiences on social media using

#PotatoChipCookingChallenge.

- Your feedback is valuable to us. If you have any suggestions or comments about our recipes or challenges, please don't hesitate to reach out.

- Thank you for joining us on this potato chip cooking journey. We hope you've been inspired to explore the wonderful world of homemade potato chips and discover endless possibilities for culinary creativity. Happy cooking!

www.ingramcontent.com/pod-product-compliance
Lightning Source LLC
Chambersburg PA
CBHW051824130726
47987CB00003B/1402